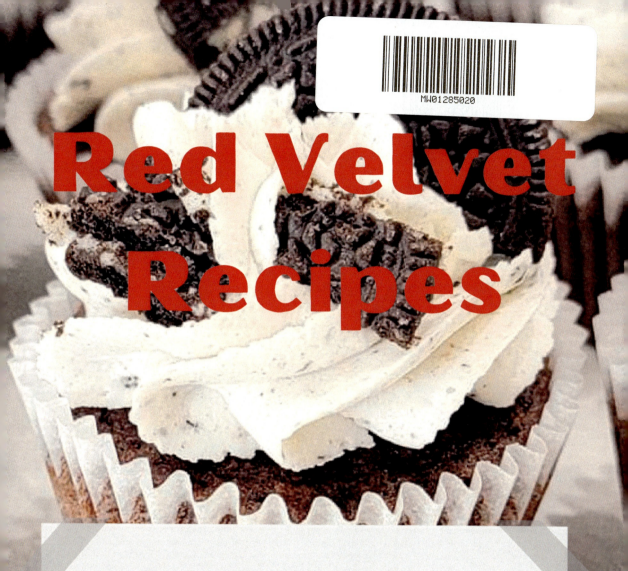

Red Velvet Recipes

ISBN: 978-1-7366811-7-6

Published by Alwayzblessd1 Creations LLC
Phoenix, AZ.

MW01285020

In memory of

1932-2019

GRANDMA GUYTON

Like most people, you consider your grandmother the best cook you know. But one secret ingredient my grandmother used in her recipes was LOVE! Nothing can compare to her love, warmth, and compassion for the entire family. The same love is shown through everything she creates. A delicious meal that can improve even your worst days is just one way you know she loves
you.

I remember the days when I would run home from school or from being out playing with my friends. The distinctive aroma floating through the air would always find a way to my nose, making my mouth water and tummy waiting to be filled with tasty treats waiting for me.

You run through the door only to be greeted by her sweet, caring smile.

First, there's the food you know will be delicious just by looking at it. Then, the steam gently rises off the
full plate inviting you to take a spoonful.

Grandma's delicious meal is waiting for you to eat every drop.

And finally, you dig in. Even though your belly is full, the delicious taste invites you to eat more.

Through every tasty mouthful, you feel the love and effort put into this deliciousness grandma made.

And then you hear:

"Are you sure you don't want more? Here, eat!"

And you say:

"No, thank you, I'm full."

Grandma:

"Only one more plate; eat it while it's still hot."

The passion and love poured into the delicious food linger in your heart even though the last time you ate it was so long ago.

Grandmother Thelma Lee Guyton knew about putting together a meal and improvising ingredients from delicious casseroles to sugary sweet Thanksgiving Day cakes and pies.

Ready for a taste of the past? Here are some cake recipes my grandma knew by heart; yours probably did too! She used a big mixing bowl, a big spoon and fork, her favorite coffee mug measuring one cup, and the one-pound box of confectioners' sugar to measure the cake flour.

To make it a little easier, I took the liberty and measured the ingredients with a measuring cup. The
recipes are simple and can make about any cake flavor. Just do not forget the buttermilk!

Enjoy eating more cake!

Red Velvet

Baking Measurements

Listed below are some U.S. customary units and their equivalent metric unit conversions.

LIQUID VOLUME CONVERSIONS

U.S. Units	Metric Units
1 teaspoon	4.93 mL
1 tablespoon	14.79 mL
1 fluid ounce	29.57 mL
1 cup	240 mL

DRY VOLUME CONVERSIONS

U.S. Units	Metric Units
1 tablespoon	14.3 g
1/8 cup	28.35 g
1/2 cup	113.4 g
4 cups	907 g

Worth Remembering

- Keep a toothbrush around the kitchen sink- you will find it helpful in cleaning rotary beaters, graters, choppers, and similar kitchen utensils.
- Dip a new broom in hot salt water before using it. This will toughen the bristles and make them last longer.
- You can easily clean darkened aluminum pans by boiling two teaspoons of cream of tartar mixed in a quart of water. Ten minutes will do it.
- Most of the time, room temperature ingredients are the best; however, it is not always necessary. For example, some recipes ask you to use cold ingredients.
- Substituting baking powder with baking soda and vice versa. That is a BIG MISTAKE... You cannot substitute baking powder with baking soda or vice versa. They both have different chemical properties.
- Weighing your ingredients is not a waste of time but essential while baking. You will always notice a change in texture and taste if you do not consider your ingredients.
- Chilling your cookie dough for an hour in the fridge or 20-25 mins in the freezer is recommended. This will always yield perfect cookies each time you bake them.
- It is best to line your baking dishes with parchment paper or butter paper before pouring the batter into them.
- Another essential step while baking is to fold the flour and not beat the flour into the batter. Beating it will lead to an over-mixed batter. The cut & fold method is popularly used to fold the dry ingredients into your cake batter.
- Once you have baked your goodies, you must cool them completely before storing them. It is imperative to wrap baked cakes in some cling wrap to avoid them from turning dry. If you plan to keep the cakes longer, it's wise to store them in the freezer than in the fridge, as storing them in the refrigerator would dry the cakes but freezing them would keep them intact.

Substitutions

- Buttermilk: 1 cup = 1 cup yogurt (not Greek) or 1 cup milk + 1 tablespoon vinegar or lemon juice; let the mixture sit until curdled before using, about 10 minutes
- Cake Flour: 1 cup = 1 cup + 2 tablespoons all-purpose flour + 2 tablespoons cornstarch
- Self-Rising Flour: 1 cup = 1 cup all-purpose flour + 1 1/2 teaspoons baking powder + 1/4 teaspoon salt
- Cream of Tartar: large pinch to 1/4 teaspoon = 1/2 teaspoon lemon juice
- Dutch Process Cocoa Powder: 1/2 cup = 1/2 cup natural cocoa + replace the baking powder in the recipe with half the amount of baking soda
- Natural Cocoa Powder: 1/2 cup = 1/2 cup Dutch process cocoa + replace the baking soda in the recipe with twice the amount of baking powder
- Eggs: 1 egg = 3 tablespoons mayonnaise or 1 tablespoon ground flaxseed and 3 tablespoons water; let sit for 5 minutes before using. Exception: Do not substitute for any recipe that uses whipped egg whites.
- Half-and-Half: 1 cup = 1/2 cup whole milk + 1/2 cup heavy cream
- Heavy Cream: 1 cup = 1 cup whole milk + 1 tablespoon melted butter
- Pumpkin Pie Spice: 1 teaspoon = 1/2 teaspoon ground cinnamon + 1/4 teaspoon ground ginger + 1/8 teaspoon ground clove + 1/8 teaspoon freshly grated nutmeg
- Iodized Salt: 1/2 teaspoon = 3/4 teaspoon kosher salt
- Kosher Salt: 1/2 teaspoon = 1/4 teaspoon iodized salt
- Semisweet Chocolate: 1 ounce = 3 tablespoons cocoa powder + 3 tablespoons granulated sugar + 1 tablespoon oil or melted butter
- Dark Brown Sugar: 1 cup = 1 cup granulated sugar + 2 tablespoons molasses or 1 cup light brown sugar
- Light Brown Sugar: 1 cup = 1 cup granulated sugar + 1 tablespoon molasses or 1 cup dark brown sugar
- Lemon Juice: 1 teaspoon = 1/2 teaspoon apple cider vinegar
- Sour Cream: 1 cup = 1 cup of plain yogurt
- Vanilla Extract: 1 teaspoon = 1 teaspoon bourbon or rum
- Whole Milk: 1 cup = 1 cup skim or low-fat milk + 2 tablespoons melted butter
- Yogurt: 1 cup = 1 cup sour cream

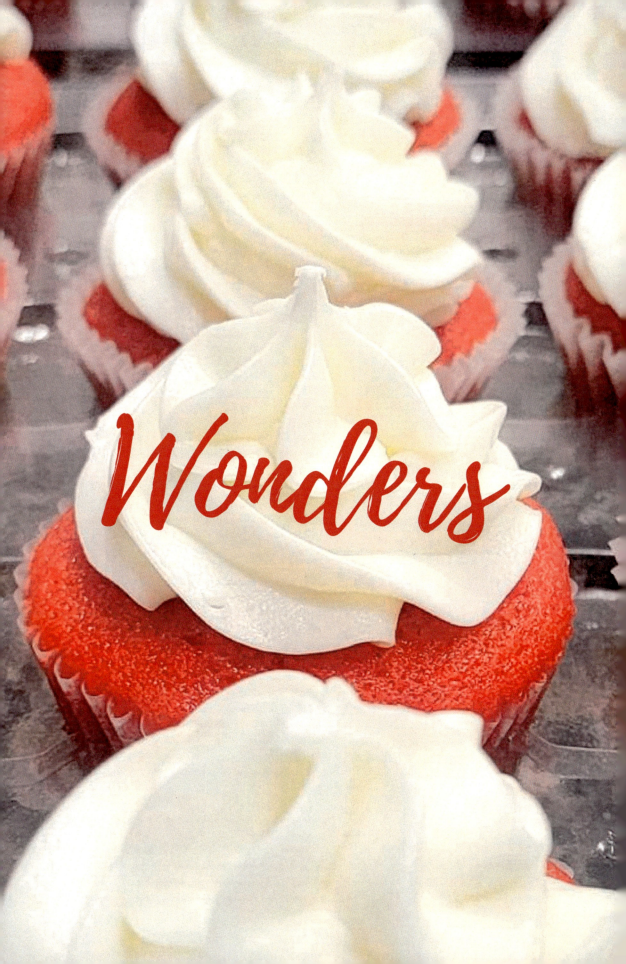

Red Velvet

🍴 **24 Cupcakes or a 3 layer 9 inch round cake**

Ingredients

Cake Mix
- 3 cups cake flour
- 2 cups sugar
- 2 teaspoons cocoa
- 2 teaspoons baking soda
- Pinch of salt
- 3 large eggs
- 1-1/2 cups vegetable oil
- 1 teaspoon vinegar
- 1-1/2 cups buttermilk
- 2 tablespoon vanilla extract
- 2 tablespoon of red food coloring

Cream Cheese Frosting
- 1 8 oz. block cream cheese, room temperature
- 3/4 cups of unsalted butter room temperature
- 1 tsp vanilla extract
- Pinch of salt
- 4 to 6 cups confectioners' sugar, sifted

Directions

For the Cake:
1. Preheat the oven to 350 degrees grease and dust with flour in three 9-inch cake pans.
2. Sift the cake flour, sugar, salt, cocoa, and baking soda into a large bowl.
3. In a small mixing bowl, blend eggs and vegetable oil. Add in the vanilla.
4. Mix the buttermilk, vinegar, and red food coloring in a liquid measuring cup. (Tip more red color the brighter the color when baked.)
5. Slowly add the wet ingredients to the dry ingredients while mixing. Mix until combined, scraping the bowl down as needed.
6. Divide the batter among the prepared pans.
7. Bake for about 30 to 35 minutes or until the centers are springy. Cool for 10 minutes before removing it from the pan.

For the Cream Cheese Frosting:
1. In a large mixing bowl or a stand mixer fitted with the paddle attachment, beat the butter and cream cheese together on medium speed until smooth and fluffy, about 3 minutes.
2. Add the vanilla and salt and beat until combined.
3. Sift the confectioner's sugar into a large bowl.
4. With the mixer on low speed, gradually add the sugar to the butter mixture until combined. Stop and scrape down the bowl occasionally. Increase speed to medium and beat until fluffy, about 1 minute.

For the Cupcakes:
1. Preheat the oven to 350 degrees. Place cupcake papers in a cupcake pan.
2. Distribute the batter evenly into cupcake papers.
3. Bake at 350 for 20-23 minutes or until springy to the touch.
4. Transfer buttercream to a piping bag fitted with a decorative tip and pipe large dollops on top of each cupcake.

Red Velvet Peppermint

🍴 24 Cupcakes or a 3 layer 9 inch round cake

Directions

For the Cake:

1. Preheat the oven to 350 degrees grease and dust with flour in three 9-inch cake pans or 24 cupcakes.

2. Sift the cake flour, sugar, salt, cocoa, and baking soda into a large bowl.

3. In a small mixing bowl, blend eggs and vegetable oil. Add in the vanilla.

4. Mix the buttermilk, vinegar, and red food coloring in a liquid measuring cup. (Tip more red color the brighter the color when baked.)

5. Slowly add the wet ingredients to the dry ingredients while mixing. Mix until combined, scraping the bowl down as needed.

6. Divide the batter among the prepared pans.

7. Bake for about 30 to 35 minutes or until the centers are springy. Cool for 10 minutes before removing it from the pan.

For the Cupcakes:

1. Preheat the oven to 350 degrees. Place cupcake papers in a cupcake pan.

2. Distribute the batter evenly into cupcake papers.

3. Bake at 350 for 20-23 minutes or until springy to the touch.

4. Transfer buttercream to a piping bag fitted with a decorative tip and pipe large dollops on top of each cupcake.

For the Buttercream Frosting:

1. In a large mixing bowl or the bowl of a stand mixer fitted with the paddle attachment, beat the butter until smooth, about 3 minutes.

2. Add the peppermint and salt and beat until combined.

3. Sift the confectioner's sugar into a large bowl.

4. Mix on low speed, and gradually add the sugar into the butter mixture until combined. Stop and scrape down the bowl occasionally. Add in heavy cream. Increase speed to medium and beat until fluffy, about 1 minute.

5. Transfer buttercream to a piping bag fitted with a decorative tip and pipe large dollops on top of each cupcake.

Ingredients

Cake Mix

- 3 cups cake flour
- 2 cups sugar
- 2 teaspoons cocoa
- 2 teaspoons baking soda
- Pinch of salt
- 3 large eggs
- 1-1/2 cups vegetable oil
- 1 teaspoon vinegar
- 1-1/2 cups buttermilk
- 2 tablespoons vanilla extract
- 2 tablespoons of red food coloring

Buttercream Frosting

- 1-1/2 cups of unsalted butter room temperature
- 2 teaspoons peppermint extract
- Pinch of salt
- 4-6 cups of confectioners' sugar, sifted
- 1/3 cup of heavy whipping cream
- Garnish with peppermint bark pieces

Vanilla Salted Caramel

Serving: 24 Cupcakes or a 3 layer 9 inch round cake

INGREDIENTS

Cake Mix

- 3 cups cake flour
- 2 cups sugar
- 2 teaspoons baking soda
- Pinch of salt
- 3 large eggs
- 1-1/2 cups vegetable oil
- 1 teaspoon vinegar
- 1-1/2 cups buttermilk
- 2 tablespoons vanilla extract

Vanilla Salted Buttercream Frosting

- 1 cup of unsalted butter at room temperature
- 2 teaspoons vanilla extract
- Pinch of salt
- 5-6 cups of confectioners' sugar
- 1 cup of caramel sauce

*Lightly sprinkle salt on top of each cupcake

Easy Caramel Sauce

- 1-1/2 cups sugar
- ¼ cup water
- 1 cup heavy cream
- 5 tablespoons unsalted butter
- ½ teaspoons salt

DIRECTIONS

For the Cupcakes:

1. Preheat the oven to 350 degrees—place cupcake papers in a cupcake pan.
2. Sift the cake flour, sugar, salt, and baking soda into a large bowl.
3. In a small mixing bowl, blend eggs and vegetable oil.
4. Mix the buttermilk, vinegar, and vanilla in a liquid measuring cup.
5. Slowly add the wet ingredients to the dry ingredients while mixing. Mix until combined, scraping the bowl down as needed.
6. Distribute the batter evenly into cupcake papers.
7. Bake at 350 degrees for 20-23 minutes or until springy to the touch.

For the Buttercream Frosting:

1. In a large mixing bowl or the bowl of a stand mixer fitted with the paddle attachment, beat the butter until smooth, about 3 minutes.
2. Add the vanilla and caramel sauce, beat until combined.
3. Sift the confectioner's sugar into a large bowl.
4. With the mixer on low speed, gradually add the sugar to the butter mixture until combined. Stop and scrape down the bowl occasionally. Increase speed to medium and beat until fluffy, about 1 minute.
5. Transfer buttercream to a piping bag fitted with a decorative tip and pipe large dollops on top of each cupcake.

Maple Walnut

Serving: 24 Cupcakes or a 3 layer 9 inch round cake

INGREDIENTS

Cake Mix

- 3 cups cake flour
- 2 cups sugar
- 2 teaspoons baking soda
- Pinch of salt
- 3 large eggs
- 1-1/2 cups vegetable oil
- 1 teaspoon vinegar
- 1-1/2 cups buttermilk
- ¼ cup maple syrup or flavor
- 1 cup chopped walnuts

Maple Buttercream Frosting

- 4-6 cups confectioners' sugar, sifted
- 1 1/2 cups of unsalted butter, room temperature
- 2 tablespoons vanilla extract
- 1/3 cup heavy cream
- Pinch of salt
- 2 tablespoons maple extract or maple syrup
- Garnish with chopped walnuts

DIRECTIONS

For the Cupcakes:

1. Preheat the oven to 350 degrees —place cupcake papers in a cupcake pan.
2. Sift together the cake flour, sugar, salt, and baking soda in a large bowl.
3. In a small mixing bowl, blend eggs and vegetable oil.
4. Mix the buttermilk, vinegar, and maple syrup in a liquid measuring cup.
5. Slowly add the wet ingredients to the dry ingredients while mixing. Mix until combined, scraping the bowl down as needed. Stir in chopped walnuts.
6. Distribute the batter evenly into cupcake papers.
7. Bake at 350 degrees for 20-23 minutes or until springy to the touch.

For the Buttercream Frosting:

1. In a large mixing bowl or the bowl of a stand mixer with the whisk attachment, whip the butter until very light and fluffy, about 5 minutes.
2. Add maple, cream, vanilla, and salt. Mix on low speed until well combined, stopping to scrape down the bowl several times. With the mixer on low, gradually add the confectioners' sugar, about a cup at a time. Scrape down the bowl.
3. Increase the speed to medium-low and beat until fluffy, about 1 minute.
4. Transfer buttercream to a piping bag fitted with a decorative tip and pipe large dollops on top of each cupcake.

Rum Raisin

Serving: 24 Cupcakes or a 3 layer 9 inch round cake

INGREDIENTS

Cake Mix

- 3 cups cake flour
- 2 cups sugar
- 2 teaspoons baking soda
- Pinch of salt
- 3 large eggs
- 1-1/2 cups vegetable oil
- 1 teaspoon vinegar
- 1-1/2 cups buttermilk
- 4 tablespoons of rum flavor
- 2-1/2 cups of raisins

Cream Cheese Frosting

- 3/4 cup of unsalted butter at room temperature
- 8 oz. block cream cheese at room temperature
- 1 teaspoon vanilla extract
- Pinch of salt
- 4-6 cups of confectioners' sugar. sifted
- Garnish with raisins and ground cinnamon

DIRECTIONS

For the Cupcake:

1. Preheat the oven to 350 degrees—place cupcake papers in a cupcake pan.
2. Sift the cake flour, sugar, salt, raisins, and baking soda into a large bowl.
3. In a small mixing bowl, blend eggs and vegetable oil.
4. Mix the buttermilk, vinegar, and rum flavor in a liquid measuring cup.
5. Slowly add the wet ingredients to the dry ingredients while mixing. Mix until combined, scraping the bowl down as needed.
6. Distribute the batter evenly into cupcake papers.
7. Bake at 350 degrees for 20-23 minutes or until springy to the touch.

For the Cream Cheese Frosting:

1. In a large mixing bowl or a stand mixer fitted with the paddle attachment, beat the butter and cream cheese together on medium speed until smooth and fluffy, about 3 minutes.
2. Add the vanilla and salt and beat until combined.
3. Sift the confectioner's sugar into a large bowl.
4. With the mixer on low speed, gradually add the sugar to the butter mixture until combined. Stop and scrape down the bowl occasionally. Increase speed to medium and beat until fluffy, about 1 minute.
5. Transfer buttercream to a piping bag fitted with a decorative tip and pipe large dollops on top of each cupcake.

Irish Cream

Serving: 24 Cupcakes or a 3 layer 9 inch round cake

INGREDIENTS

Cake Mix

- 3 cups cake flour
- 2 cups sugar
- 3 tablespoons of dark cocoa
- 2 teaspoons baking soda
- Pinch of salt
- 3 large eggs
- 1-1/2 cups vegetable oil
- 1 teaspoon vinegar
- 2 cups buttermilk

Buttercream Frosting

- 4-6 cups confectioners' sugar. sifted
- 1 1/2 cups of unsalted butter
- 2 tablespoons vanilla extract
- 1/3 cup heavy cream
- Pinch of salt
- 2 tablespoons of Irish cream

DIRECTIONS

For the Cupcakes:

1. Preheat the oven to 350 degrees —place cupcake papers in a cupcake pan.
2. Sift the cake flour, sugar, salt, cocoa, and baking soda into a large bowl.
3. In a small mixing bowl, blend eggs and vegetable oil. Add in buttermilk and vinegar
4. Slowly add the wet ingredients to the dry ingredients while mixing. Mix until combined, scraping the bowl down as needed.
5. Distribute the batter evenly into cupcake papers.
6. Bake at 350 degrees for 20-23 minutes or until springy to the touch.

For the Buttercream Frosting:

1. In a large mixing bowl or a stand mixer fitted with the paddle attachment, beat the butter until smooth, about 3 minutes.
2. Add the Irish Cream flavor, vanilla, and salt and beat until combined.
3. Sift the confectioner's sugar into a large bowl.
4. With the mixer on low speed, gradually add the sugar to the butter mixture until combined. Stop and scrape down the bowl occasionally. Add in heavy cream. Increase speed to medium and beat until fluffy, about 1 minute.
5. Transfer buttercream to a piping bag fitted with a decorative tip and pipe large dollops on top of each cupcake.

Vanilla Chocolate
Raspberry

VANILLA CHOCOLATE RASPBERRY

Serving: 24 Cupcakes or a 3 layer 9 inch round cake

Ingredients

Cake Mix
- 3 cups cake flour
- 2 cups sugar
- 2 teaspoons baking soda
- Pinch of salt
- 3 large eggs
- 1-1/2 cups vegetable oil
- 1 teaspoon vinegar
- 1-1/2 cups buttermilk
- 2 tablespoon raspberry flavor

Chocolate Buttercream Frosting
- 1-1/2 cups of unsalted butter room temperature
- ½ cup of unsweetened cocoa
- ¾ teaspoon of salt
- 1-1/2 teaspoons vanilla extract
- 6-8 cups of confectioners sugar
- ½ cup of heavy whipping cream
- Garnish with fresh raspberry

Directions

For the Cupcakes:
1. Preheat the oven to 350 degrees—place cupcake papers in a cupcake pan.
2. Sift the cake flour, sugar, salt, and baking soda into a large bowl.
3. In a small mixing bowl, blend eggs and vegetable oil.
4. Mix the buttermilk, vinegar, and raspberry flavor in a liquid measuring cup.
5. Slowly add the wet ingredients to the dry ingredients while mixing. Mix until combined, scraping the bowl down as needed.
6. Distribute the batter evenly into cupcake papers.
7. Bake at 350 degrees for 20-23 minutes or until springy to the touch.

For the Chocolate Buttercream Frosting:
1. In a large mixing bowl or the bowl of a stand mixer with the whisk attachment, whip the butter until very light and fluffy, about 5 minutes.
2. Add the cocoa, vanilla, cream, and salt. Mix on low speed until well combined, stopping to scrape down the bowl several times. With the mixer on low, gradually add the confectioners' sugar, about a cup, alternating with a tablespoon of cream. 6 cups of sugar for a smooth and swoopy frosting but a stiffer frosting; use up to 8 cups of sugar.) Scrape down the bowl.
3. Increase the speed to medium-low and beat until fluffy and spreadable, about 1 minute.
4. Transfer buttercream to a piping bag fitted with a decorative tip and pipe large dollops on top of each cupcake.

RECIPE CARD

INGREDIENTS:

_____
_____
_____
_____
_____
_____
_____
_____
_____
_____
_____
_____
_____
_____
_____
_____
_____
_____

DIRECTIONS:

_____
_____
_____
_____
_____
_____
_____
_____
_____
_____
_____
_____
_____
_____
_____
_____
_____
_____
_____

Serves   **prep**   **cook**

Notes

RECIPE CARD

INGREDIENTS:

DIRECTIONS:

Serves   prep   cook

Notes

STRAWBERRY KEY-LIME

Serving: 24 Cupcakes or a 3 layer 9 inch round cake

Ingredients

Cake Mix
- 3 cups cake flour
- 2 cups sugar
- 4 tablespoons of key lime juice
- 2 tablespoons strawberry flavor
- 2 teaspoons baking soda
- Pinch of salt
- 3 large eggs
- 1-1/2 cups vegetable oil
- 1 teaspoon vinegar
- 1 1/2 cups buttermilk
- 2 tablespoons of pink food coloring

Buttercream
- 4-6 cups confectioners' sugar. sifted
- 1 1/2 cups of unsalted butter
- 2 tablespoons vanilla extract
- 1/3 cup of heavy cream
- Pinch of salt
- Garnish with strawberry & key lime crumble

Strawberry and Lime Crumble
- (2)1/4 cup flour
- ½ cup of butter; room temperature
- 3-ounce box of Strawberry flavor jello
- 3-ounce box of Lime flavor jello

Directions

For the Cupcake:
1. Preheat the oven to 350 degrees — place cupcake papers in a cupcake pan.
2. Sift the cake flour, sugar, salt, and baking soda into a large bowl.
3. In a small mixing bowl, blend eggs, vegetable oil, buttermilk, key lime juice, strawberry flavor, pink food coloring, and vinegar.
4. Slowly add the wet ingredients to the dry ingredients while mixing. Scrape the bowl down as needed.
5. Distribute the batter evenly into cupcake papers.
6. Bake at 350 for 20-23 minutes or until springy to the touch.

For the Buttercream Frosting:
1. In a large mixing bowl or the bowl of a stand mixer with the whisk attachment, whip the butter until very light and fluffy, about 5 minutes.
2. Add vanilla and cream. Mix on low speed until well combined, stopping to scrape down the bowl several times. With the mixer on low, gradually add in the confectioners' sugar, about a cup at a time— scrape down the bowl.
3. Increase the speed to medium-low and beat until fluffy is about 1 minute.
4. Transfer buttercream to a piping bag fitted with a decorative tip and pipe large dollops on top of each cupcake.

For Crumble:
1. Preheat the oven to 350 degrees
2. 1/4 stick of butter in each bowl, ¼ cup of flour in each bowl, one jello flavor per bowl
3. Mix with a fork until clumpy.
4. Using gloves, roll out jello on the baking pan with parchment paper.
5. Mix the two flavors of jello with your hands; it should look marbly and roll thin.
6. Bake for 6-8 minutes. Check at 6 minutes; overcooking will burn the jello
7. Let it cool on a cooling rack for 1 hour, then put it in the refrigerator for 30 minutes, break up the jello, and place it in a food processor. Do not over-blend, or it will turn into powder.

STRAWBERRY CRUMBLE

Serving : 24 Cupcakes or a 3 layer 9 inch round cake

Ingredients

Cake Mix
- 3 cups cake flour
- 2 cups sugar
- 2 teaspoons baking soda
- Pinch of salt
- 3 large eggs
- 1-1/2 cups vegetable oil
- 1 teaspoon vinegar
- 1-1/2 cups buttermilk
- 2 tablespoons of pink food coloring
- 2 tablespoons of strawberry flavor

Cream Cheese Frosting
- 8 oz. of room-temperature cream cheese
- 3/4 cup of unsalted butter at room temperature
- 1 tsp vanilla extract
- Pinch of salt
- 4 to 6 cups confectioners sugar sifted
- 2-4 drops of pink food color (optional)
- Garnish with Strawberry Crumble

Strawberry Crumble
- Vanilla pudding mix, 3 oz box
- Strawberry jello 3 oz box
- 1 stick of butter, room temperature
- 2-1/4 cups of flour

Directions

For the Cupcake:
1. Preheat the oven to 350 degrees —place cupcake papers in a cupcake pan.
2. Sift the cake flour, sugar, salt, and baking soda into a large bowl.
3. In a small mixing bowl, blend eggs and vegetable oil.
4. Mix the buttermilk, vinegar, strawberry flavor, and pink color in a liquid measuring cup.
5. Slowly add the wet ingredients to the dry ingredients while mixing. Mix until combined, scraping the bowl down as needed.
6. Distribute the batter evenly into cupcake papers.
7. Bake at 350 degrees for 20-23 minutes or until springy to the touch.

Buttercream Frosting:
1. In a large mixing bowl or the bowl of a stand mixer with the whisk attachment, whip the butter and cream cheese until very light and fluffy, about 5 minutes.
2. Add strawberry flavor, pink food coloring, vanilla, cream, and salt. Mix on low speed until well combined, stopping to scrape down the bowl several times. With the mixer on low, gradually add the confectioners' sugar, about a cup at a time. (I like 6 cups of sugar for a smooth and swoopy frosting, but I use up to 8 cups of sugar for a stiffer frosting.) Scrape down the bowl.
3. Increase the speed to medium-low and beat until fluffy and spreadable, about 1 minute.
4. Transfer buttercream to a piping bag fitted with a decorative tip and pipe large dollops on top of each cupcake.

Strawberry Crumble
1. Preheat the oven to 350 degrees
2. In two separate bowls, add 1/4 stick of butter, ¼ cup of flour, and one package of Strawberry flavor jello in one bowl and vanilla pudding mix in the other.
3. Fork mixture together evenly and until clumpy.
4. Using gloves, roll out the baking sheet pan with parchment paper. It should be thin.
5. Bake for 6-8 minutes. Check at 6 minutes; overcooking will burn the jello
6. Let it cool on a cooling rack for 1 hour, then put it in the refrigerator for 30 minutes, break up the jello, and place it in a food processor. Do not over-blend, or it will turn into powder.

Peach Cobbler

Sour Apple

Serving : 24 Cupcakes or a 3 layer 9 inch round cake

INGREDIENTS

Cake Mix
- 3 cups cake flour
- 2 cups sugar
- 2 teaspoons baking soda
- Pinch of salt
- 3 large eggs
- 1-1/2 cups vegetable oil
- 1 teaspoon vinegar
- 1-1/2 cups buttermilk
- 4 tablespoons green apple flavor

Optional use 1 drop of leaf green food color

Buttercream Frosting
- 4-6 cups of confectioners' sugar, sifted
- 1 1/2 cups of unsalted butter. room temperature
- 2 tablespoons vanilla extract
- 1/3 cup heavy cream
- Pinch of salt
- Garnish with caramel sauce and a fresh slice of green apple.

Salted Caramel Sauce
- ¼ cup water
- 1 cup granulated sugar
- 2/3 cup heavy whipping cream
- 3 tablespoons unsalted butter
- 1 teaspoon vanilla extract
- 1 teaspoon salt

DIRECTIONS

For the Cupcake:

1. Preheat the oven to 350 degrees —place cupcake papers in a cupcake pan.
2. Sift the cake flour, sugar, salt, and baking soda into a large bowl.
3. In a small mixing bowl, blend eggs and vegetable oil.
4. Mix the buttermilk, vinegar, and green apple flavor in a liquid measuring cup.
5. Slowly add the wet ingredients to the dry ingredients while mixing. Mix until combined, scraping the bowl down as needed.
6. Distribute the batter evenly into cupcake papers.
7. Bake at 350F for 20-23 minutes or until springy to the touch.

For the Buttercream Frosting:

1. In a large mixing bowl or the bowl of a stand mixer with the whisk attachment, whip the butter until very light and fluffy, about 5 minutes.
2. Add vanilla, cream, and salt. Mix on low speed until well combined, stopping to scrape down the bowl several times. With the mixer on low, gradually add the confectioners' sugar, about a cup at a time. Scrape down the bowl.
3. Increase the speed to medium-low and beat until fluffy, about 1 minute.
4. Transfer buttercream to a piping bag fitted with a decorative tip and piped large dollops on top of each cupcake.

Peach Cobbler

Serving : 24 Cupcakes or a 3 layer 9 inch round cake

INGREDIENTS

Cake Mix
- 3 cups cake flour
- 2 cups sugar
- 2 teaspoons baking soda
- Pinch of salt
- 3 large eggs
- 1-1/2 cups vegetable oil
- 1 teaspoon vinegar
- 1-1/2 cups buttermilk
- 2 tablespoon peach flavor

Cream Cheese Frosting
- 1 8 oz. block of cream cheese at room temperature
- 3/4 cup of unsalted butter at room temperature
- 1 tsp vanilla extract
- Pinch of salt
- 4 to 6 cups confectioners sugar sifted
- Garnish with sliced peaches, and pie crumble

Pie Crumble
- 1 cup flour
- 1/3 cup white sugar
- 1/3 cup brown sugar packed
- ½ teaspoon cinnamon
- 1/8 teaspoon ground ginger
- ¼ teaspoon salt or to taste
- ½ cup unsalted butter cold, cut into cubes

DIRECTIONS

For the Cupcakes:

1. Preheat the oven to 350 degrees —place cupcake papers in a cupcake pan.
2. Sift the cake flour, sugar, salt, and baking soda into a large bowl.
3. In a small mixing bowl, blend eggs and vegetable oil.
4. Mix the buttermilk, vinegar, and peach flavor in a liquid measuring cup.
5. Slowly add the wet ingredients to the dry ingredients while mixing. Mix until combined, scraping the bowl down as needed.
6. Distribute the batter evenly into cupcake papers.
7. Bake at 350F for 20-23 minutes or until springy to the touch.

For the Cream Cheese Frosting:

1. In a large mixing bowl or a stand mixer fitted with the paddle attachment, beat the butter and cream cheese together on medium speed until smooth and fluffy, about 3 minutes.
2. Add the vanilla and salt and beat until combined.
3. Sift the confectioner's sugar into a large bowl.
4. Slowly add confectioners' sugar on low speed till combined with butter. Stop and scrape down the bowl occasionally. Increase speed to medium and beat until fluffy, about 1 minute.

Pie Crumble:

1. Preheat the oven to 350 degrees.
2. Place all ingredients in a medium bowl. Use a pastry cutter to cut in cold butter until the mixture starts to stick together, about 3 minutes.
3. Take the mixture and roll it out.
4. Bake for 10-12 minutes, let cool for 1 hour, refrigerate for 30 minutes, and use gloves to crumble into medium and large pieces.

Vanilla
Strawberry

FRUITY TOOTIE PEBBLE

Serving : 24 Cupcakes or a 3 layer 9 inch round cake

Ingredients

Cake Mix
- 3 cups cake flour
- 1 cup fruity pebbles
- 2 cups sugar
- 2 teaspoons baking soda
- Pinch of salt
- 3 large eggs
- 1-1/2 cups vegetable oil
- 1 teaspoon vinegar
- 1-1/2 cups buttermilk

Buttercream Frosting-
- 4-6 cups confectioners' sugar. sifted
- 1 1/2 cups of unsalted butter, room temperature
- 2 tablespoons vanilla extract
- 1/3 cup heavy cream
- Pinch of salt
- Garnish with fruity pebble cereal

Directions

For the Cupcakes:
1. Preheat the oven to 350 degrees — place cupcake papers in a cupcake pan.
2. Sift the cake flour, fruity pebbles, sugar, salt, and baking soda into a large bowl.
3. In a small mixing bowl, blend eggs and vegetable oil.
4. Mix the buttermilk and vinegar, in a liquid measuring cup.
5. Slowly add the wet ingredients to the dry ingredients while mixing. Mix until combined, scraping the bowl down as needed.
6. Distribute the batter evenly into cupcake papers.
7. Bake at 350 degrees for 20-23 minutes or until springy to the touch.

For the Buttercream Frosting:
1. In a large mixing bowl or the bowl of a stand mixer with the whisk attachment, whip the butter until very light and fluffy, about 5 minutes.
2. Add vanilla, cream, and salt. Mix on low speed until well combined, stopping to scrape down the bowl several times. With the mixer on low, gradually add the confectioners' sugar about a cup at a time. Scrape down the bowl.
3. Increase the speed to medium-low and beat until fluffy , about 1 minute.
4. Transfer buttercream to a piping bag fitted with a decorative tip and pipe large dollops on top of each cupcake.

BLACKBERRY

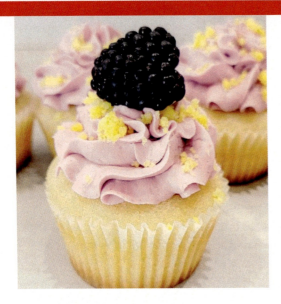

Ingredients

Cake Mix
- 3 cups cake flour
- 2 cups sugar
- 2 teaspoons baking soda
- Pinch of salt
- 3 large eggs
- 1-1/2 cups vegetable oil
- 1 teaspoon vinegar
- 1-1/2 cups buttermilk
- 2 tablespoon blackberry flavoring

Blackberry Cream Cheese Frosting
- ½ cup butter, room temperature
- 1-1/2 cup confectioners' sugar
- Pinch of salt
- 8 oz. of cream cheese at room temperature
- 6 ounces of blackberries (puree)
- ½ teaspoon of vanilla extract
- Garnish with fresh blackberry

Directions

For the Cupcakes:
1. Preheat the oven to 350 degrees. Place cupcake papers in a cupcake pan.
2. Sift together the cake flour, sugar, salt, and baking soda in a large bowl.
3. In a small mixing bowl, blend eggs and vegetable oil.
4. Mix the buttermilk, vinegar, and blackberry flavor in a liquid measuring cup.
5. Slowly add the wet ingredients to the dry ingredients while mixing. Mix until combined, scraping the bowl down as needed.
6. Distribute the batter evenly into cupcake papers.
7. Bake at 350 degrees for 20-23 minutes or until springy to the touch.

For the Blackberry Cream Cheese Frosting:
1. In a large mixing bowl or the bowl of a stand mixer fitted with the paddle attachment, beat the butter and cream cheese together on medium speed until smooth and fluffy, about 3 minutes.
2. Add the vanilla, blackberry puree, and salt and beat until combined.
3. Mix the confectioner's sugar into a large bowl.
4. With the mixer on low speed, gradually add the sugar into the butter mixture until combined. Stop and scrape down the bowl occasionally. Increase speed to medium and beat until fluffy, about 1 minute.

Vanilla Sprinkle

RECIPE CARD

INGREDIENTS:

_____
_____
_____
_____
_____
_____
_____
_____
_____
_____
_____
_____
_____
_____
_____
_____
_____
_____
_____

DIRECTIONS:

_____
_____
_____
_____
_____
_____
_____
_____
_____
_____
_____
_____
_____
_____
_____
_____
_____
_____
_____
_____
_____
_____
_____
_____

Serves   **prep**   **cook**

Notes

RECIPE CARD

INGREDIENTS:

_____
_____
_____
_____
_____
_____
_____
_____
_____
_____
_____
_____
_____
_____
_____
_____
_____
_____

Serves **prep** **cook**

DIRECTIONS:

_____
_____
_____
_____
_____
_____
_____
_____
_____
_____
_____
_____
_____
_____
_____
_____
_____
_____
_____
_____

Notes

SUMMER

Lemon with Strawberry crumble

SWEETS

Red, White & Boom!

LEMON

Ingredients

Cake Mix

- 3 cups cake flour
- 2 cups sugar
- 2 teaspoons baking soda
- Pinch of salt
- 3 large eggs
- 1-1/2 cups vegetable oil
- 1 teaspoon vinegar
- 1-1/2 cups buttermilk
- ¼ cup lemon flavor or ¼ cup of lemon juice
- 3 tablespoons of lemon zest
- 2-3 drops of lemon-yellow color

Buttercream Frosting

- 4-6 cups confectioners' sugar, sifted
- 1 1/2 cups of unsalted butter, room temperature
- 2 tablespoons vanilla extract
- 1/3 cup heavy cream
- Pinch of salt
- 2 tablespoons lemon flavor
- Garnish with lemon zest (optional)

Directions

For the Cupcake:

1. Preheat the oven to 350 degrees place cupcake papers in a cupcake pan.
2. Sift the cake flour, sugar, salt, and baking soda into a large bowl.
3. In a small mixing bowl, blend eggs, vegetable oil, lemon flavor, lemon zest and yellow color. Next, add buttermilk and vinegar.
4. Slowly add the wet ingredients to the dry ingredients while mixing. Mix until combined, scraping the bowl down as needed.
5. Distribute the batter evenly into cupcake papers.
6. Bake at 350 degrees for 20-23 minutes or until springy to the touch.

For the Buttercream Frosting:

1. In a large mixing bowl or the bowl of a stand mixer with the whisk attachment, whip the butter until very light and fluffy, about 5 minutes.
2. Add lemon flavor and cream. Mix on low speed until well combined, stopping to scrape down the bowl several times.
3. Increase the speed to medium-low and beat until fluffy about 1 minute.
4. Transfer buttercream to a piping bag fitted with a decorative tip and pipe large dollops on top of each cupcake.

LEMON KEY-LIME

Serving : 24 Cupcakes or a 3 layer 9 inch round cake

Ingredients

Cake Mix
- 3 cups cake flour
- 2 cups sugar
- 4 tablespoons of key lime juice
- 2 tablespoons lemon flavor or lemon juice
- 2 teaspoons baking soda
- Pinch of salt
- 3 large eggs
- 1-1/2 cups vegetable oil
- 1 teaspoon vinegar
- 1 1/2 cups buttermilk

Buttercream
- 4-6 cups confectioners' sugar. sifted
- 1/1/2 cups of unsalted butter, room temperature
- 2 tablespoons vanilla extract
- 1/3 cup heavy cream
- Pinch of salt
- Garnish with lemon and lime crumble

Lemon and Lime Crumble
- 2- 1/4 cup flour
- ½ cup of butter; room temperature
- 3-ounce box of Lime flavor jello
- 3-ounce box of Lemon flavor jello

Directions

For the Cupcake:
1. Preheat the oven to 350 degrees —place cupcake papers in a cupcake pan.
2. Sift the cake flour, sugar, salt, and baking soda into a large bowl.
3. In a small mixing bowl, blend eggs and vegetable oil.
4. Mix the buttermilk, vinegar, and lemon flavor and key-lime juice in a liquid measuring cup.
5. Slowly add the wet ingredients to the dry ingredients while mixing. Mix until combined, scraping the bowl down as needed.
6. Distribute the batter evenly into cupcake papers.
7. Bake at 350 degrees for 20-23 minutes or until springy to the touch.

For the Buttercream Frosting:
1. In a large mixing bowl or the bowl of a stand mixer with the whisk attachment, whip the butter until very light and fluffy, about 5 minutes.
2. Add cream, vanilla and salt. Mix on low speed until well combined, stopping to scrape down the bowl several times. With the mixer on low, gradually add the confectioners' sugar, about a cup at a time. Scrape down the bowl.
3. Increase the speed to medium-low and beat until fluffy about 1 minute.
4. Transfer buttercream to a piping bag fitted with a decorative tip and pipe large dollops on top of each cupcake.

For Crumble
1. Preheat the oven to 350 degrees
2. Mix 1/4 stick of butter in each bowl, ¼ cup of flour in each bowl, and one jello flavor per bowl
3. Fork mixture together evenly and until clumpy.
4. Using gloves, roll out the baking sheet pan with parchment paper. Mix the two flavors of jello with your hands; it should look marbly; flatten it out. It should be thin.
5. Bake for 6-8 minutes. Check at 6 minutes; overcooking will burn the jello
6. Let it cool on a cooling rack for 1 hour, then put it in the refrigerator for 30 minutes, break up jello, and place it in a food processor. Do not over-blend, or it will turn into powder.

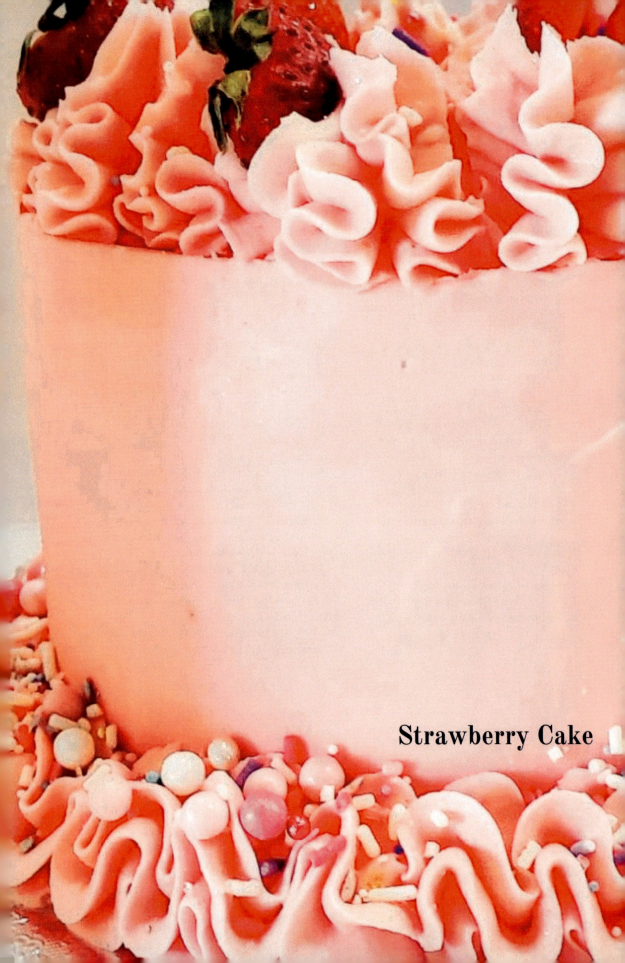

Strawberry Cake

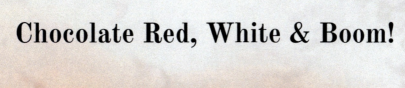

Chocolate Red, White & Boom!

Directions

For the Cupcake:
1. Preheat the oven to 350 degrees — place cupcake papers in a cupcake pan.
2. Sift the cake flour, sugar, cinnamon, salt, and baking soda into a large bowl.
3. In a small mixing bowl, blend eggs, churro flavor and vegetable oil in buttermilk and vinegar.
4. Slowly add the wet ingredients to the dry ingredients while mixing. Mix until combined, scraping the bowl down as needed.
5. Distribute the batter evenly into cupcake papers.
6. Bake at 350 degrees for 20-23 minutes or until springy to the touch.

For the Buttercream Frosting:
1. In a large mixing bowl or the bowl of a stand mixer with the whisk attachment, whip the butter until very light and fluffy, about 5 minutes.
2. Add cream and vanilla. Mix on low speed until well combined, stopping to scrape down the bowl several times. With the mixer on low, gradually add the confectioner's sugar, about a cup at a time. I like 6 cups of sugar for a smooth and swoopy frosting, but for a stiffer frosting, use up to 8 cups of sugar.) Scrape the sides of the bowl.
3. Increase the speed to medium-low and beat until fluffy and spreadable, about 1 minute.
4. Transfer buttercream to a piping bag fitted with a decorative tip and pipe large dollops on top of each cupcake.

For the Churro:
1. In a large saucepan, bring the water, butter, salt, and sugar to a rolling boil over medium-high heat. When it boils, immediately take the pan off the heat.
2. Stirring with a wooden spoon, add all the cake flour and mix till combined.
3. Return to the heat and cook for 30 seconds. Scrape the mixture into a mixer fitted with a paddle attachment (or use a hand mixer).
4. Mix at medium speed. Add eggs one at a time, then vanilla until fully incorporated. Stop mixing after each addition to scrape down the sides of the bowl. Until the dough is smooth and glossy, it should be thick but fall slowly and steadily from the beaters when you lift them out of the bowl. If the dough clings to the beaters, add the remaining egg and mix until incorporated.
5. Heat oil to 370 degrees
6. Use a pastry bag fitted with a large star tip.
7. Pipe 6-inch pieces using a large closed star tip. T's best to fry about three at a time.
8. Fry on either side for 90 seconds to 2 minutes or until golden brown.
9. Remove with tongs and allow to drain on a paper towel for about thirty seconds before placing in the cinnamon sugar. Spoon sugar over, remove excess, and serve.

CHURRO

Serving : 24 Cupcakes or a 3 layer 9 inch round cake

Ingredients

Cake Mix
- 3 cups cake flour
- 2 cups sugar
- 2 teaspoons baking soda
- Pinch of salt
- 3 large eggs
- 1-1/2 cups vegetable oil
- 1 teaspoon vinegar
- 1-1/2 cups buttermilk
- ¼ cup churro flavor
- 1 teaspoon of ground cinnamon

Cinnamon sugar mixture
- ¾ cup sugar
- 2 teaspoon cinnamon

Buttercream Frosting
- 4-6 cups of confectioners' sugar, sifted
- 1 1/2 cups unsalted butter, room temperature
- 2 tablespoons vanilla extract
- 1/3 cup heavy cream
- Pinch of salt
- Sprinkle with cinnamon sugar and top with fresh churro

Churro
- 1 cup water
- 6 tablespoons unsalted butter
- 1 tablespoon of granulated sugar
- ½ teaspoon salt
- 1 cup cake flour
- 3 large eggs
- 1 tsp vanilla extract
- Vegetable oil for frying

NEAPOLITAN

 Serving : 24 Cupcakes or a 3 layer 9 inch round cake

Ingredients

Cake Mix
- 3 cups cake flour
- 2 cups sugar
- 2 teaspoons baking soda
- Pinch of salt
- 3 large eggs
- 1-1/2 cups vegetable oil
- 1 teaspoon vinegar
- 1-1/2 cups buttermilk
- 2 tablespoons of strawberry flavor
- 2 tablespoons of pink coloring

Neapolitan Crumble
- 3- 1/4 cup flour
- 3/4 cup of butter; room temperature
- 3-ounce box of Strawberry flavor jello
- 3.4-ounce box of Vanilla flavor pudding/pie filling flavor jello
- 3.9-ounce box of Chocolate flavor pudding/pie filling jello

Vanilla & Strawberry Buttercream
- 4-6 cups confectioners' sugar, sifted
- 1 1/2 cups of unsalted butter, room temperature
- 2 tablespoons vanilla extract
- 1/3 cup heavy cream
- Pinch of salt
- Strawberry flavor

Chocolate Buttercream Frosting
- 1-1/2 cups of unsalted butter at room temperature
- ½ cup of unsweetened cocoa
- ¾ teaspoon of salt
- 1-1/2 teaspoons vanilla extract
- 6-8 cups of confectioners' sugar, sifted
- ½ cup of heavy whipping cream

Directions

For the Cupcake:
1. Preheat the oven to 350 degrees —place cupcake papers in a cupcake pan.
2. Sift the cake flour, sugar, salt, and baking soda into a large bowl.
3. In a small mixing bowl, blend eggs and vegetable oil.
4. Mix the buttermilk, vinegar, strawberry flavor, and pink color in a liquid measuring cup.
5. Slowly add the wet ingredients to the dry ingredients while mixing. Mix until combined, scraping the bowl down as needed.
6. Distribute the batter evenly into cupcake papers.
7. Bake at 350 degrees for 20-23 minutes or until springy to the touch.

For the Butter Cream Frostings:
1. Whip the butter for about 5 minutes using a paddle attachment (stand-up mixer).
2. Mix in the confectioner's sugar slowly.
3. Add the cream and vanilla. Beat until you have an even, fluffy consistency.
4. Divide buttercream into three 3 parts.
5. Transfer one vanilla batch to a piping bag and snip off the tip. For Chocolate Buttercream:
6. Mix cocoa into one batch of buttercream.
7. Transfer to a piping bag and pipe vanilla in the middle and chocolate on the right.

For the Strawberry Buttercream:
1. Add the rest of the strawberry mixture to a buttercream batch.
2. Add a few drops of pink food coloring if you want the color to be more vibrant.
3. Mix until desired consistency.
4. Transfer to a piping bag and pipe on the left side.

For Neapolitan Crumble
1. Preheat the oven to 350 degrees
2. 1/4 stick of butter in each bowl, ¼ cup of flour in each bowl, one jello flavor per bowl
3. Fork mixture together evenly and until clumpy; note that vanilla and chocolate pudding will have a doughier look than the strawberry
4. Using gloves, roll out the baking sheet pan with parchment paper. Mix the three flavors of jello with your hands; it should look marbly, and flatten it out. It should be thin.
5. Bake for 6-8 minutes. Check at 6 minutes; overcooking will burn the jello
6. Let it cool on a cooling rack for 1 hour, then put it in the refrigerator for 30 minutes.
7. Break up jello and place it in a food processor. Do not over-blend, or it will turn into powder.

Carrot-Pineapple

INGREDIENTS

Cake:

- 3 cups of cake flour
- 2 cups of sugar
- 3 eggs
- 1-1/3 cups vegetable oil
- 2 teaspoons of baking powder
- 2 teaspoons of baking soda
- 2 teaspoon ground cinnamon
- 1 teaspoon salt
- 1-1/3 cups of shredded carrots
- 1 cup of crushed pineapple (with syrup)
- 2 teaspoons vanilla extract

Cream Cheese Frosting

- 1 8 oz. block of cream cheese, room temperature
- 3/4 cup of unsalted butter, room temperature
- 1 tsp vanilla extract
- Pinch of salt
- 4 to 6 cups confectioners' sugar, sifted

DIRECTIONS

For the Cupcake:

1. Preheat the oven to 350 degrees —place cupcake papers in a cupcake pan.
2. Sift the cake flour, sugar, salt, baking powder, baking soda, cinnamon, shredded carrots, and crushed pineapple in a large bowl.
3. In a small mixing bowl, blend eggs and vegetable oil.
4. Mix the vinegar and vanilla flavor in a liquid measuring cup.
5. Slowly add the wet ingredients to the dry ingredients while mixing. Mix until combined, scraping the bowl down as needed.
6. Distribute the batter evenly into cupcake papers.
7. Bake at 350 degrees for 20-23 minutes or until springy to the touch.

For the Cream Cheese Frosting:

1. In a large mixing bowl or the bowl of a stand mixer with the whisk attachment, whip the butter and cream cheese until very light and fluffy, about 5 minutes.
2. Add vanilla and salt. Mix on low speed until well combined, stopping to scrape down the bowl several times. With the mixer on low, gradually add the confectioners' sugar, about a cup at a time. Scrape down the bowl.
3. Increase the speed to medium-low and beat until fluffy, about 1 minute.
4. Transfer frosting to a piping bag fitted with a decorative tip and pipe large dollops on top of each cupcake.

Coconut

INGREDIENTS

Cake Mix

- 3 cups cake flour
- 2 cups sugar
- 2 teaspoons baking soda
- Pinch of salt
- 3 large eggs
- 1-1/2 cups vegetable oil
- 1 teaspoon vinegar
- 1-1/2 cups buttermilk
- ¼ cup coconut flavor

Buttercream Frosting

- 4-6 cups of confectioners' sugar, sifted
- 1 1/2 cups of unsalted butter, room temperature
- 2 tablespoons vanilla extract
- 1/3 cup heavy cream
- Pinch of salt
- 7 ounces of sweetened coconut for garnish

DIRECTIONS

For the Cupcake:

1. Preheat the oven to 350 degrees — place cupcake papers in a cupcake pan.
2. Sift the cake flour, sugar, salt, and baking soda into a large bowl.
3. In a small mixing bowl, blend eggs, coconut flavor, and vegetable oil. Next, add buttermilk and vinegar.
4. Slowly add the wet ingredients to the dry ingredients while mixing. Mix until combined, scraping the bowl down as needed.
5. Distribute the batter evenly into cupcake papers.
6. Bake at 350 degrees for 20-23 minutes or until springy to the touch.

For the Buttercream Frosting:

1. In a large mixing bowl or the bowl of a stand mixer with the whisk attachment, whip the butter until very light and fluffy, about 5 minutes.
2. Add vanilla and cream, and mix on low speed until well combined, stopping to scrape down the bowl several times. With the mixer on low, gradually add in the confectioners' sugar, about a cup at a time. Scrape sides down.
3. Increase the speed to medium-low and beat until fluffy, about 1 minute.
4. Transfer buttercream to a piping bag fitted with a decorative tip and pipe large dollops on top of each cupcake.

Chocolate S'mores

Serving : 24 Cupcakes or a 3 layer 9 inch round cake

INGREDIENTS

Cake Mix

- 3 cups cake flour
- 2 cups sugar
- 3 tablespoons of dark cocoa
- 2 teaspoons baking soda
- Pinch of salt
- 3 large eggs
- 1-1/2 cups vegetable oil
- 1 teaspoon vinegar
- 2 cups buttermilk

Buttercream Frosting

- 4-6 cups of confectioners' sugar, sifted
- 1 1/2 cups of unsalted butter, room temperature
- 2 tablespoons vanilla extract
- 1/3 cup heavy cream
- Pinch of salt
- Garnish with mini marshmallows, crushed graham crackers, chocolate syrup, and chocolate candy

DIRECTIONS

For the Cupcakes:

1. Preheat the oven to 350 degrees —place cupcake papers in a cupcake pan.
2. Sift the cake flour, sugar, salt, cocoa, and baking soda into a large bowl.
3. In a small mixing bowl, blend eggs and vegetable oil.
4. Mix the buttermilk and vinegar in a liquid measuring cup.
5. Slowly add the wet ingredients to the dry ingredients while mixing. Mix until combined, scraping the bowl down as needed.
6. Distribute the batter evenly into cupcake papers.
7. Bake at 350 degrees for 20-23 minutes or until springy to the touch.

For the Buttercream Frosting:

1. In a large mixing bowl or the bowl of a stand mixer with the whisk attachment, whip the butter until very light and fluffy, about 5 minutes.
2. Add vanilla, cream, and salt. Mix on low speed until well combined, stopping to scrape down the bowl several times. With the mixer on low, gradually add in the confectioners' sugar, about a cup at a time—scrape the sides of the bowl.
3. Increase the speed to medium-low and beat until fluffy, about 1 minute.
4. Transfer buttercream to a piping bag fitted with a decorative tip and pipe large dollops on top of each cupcake.

Cotton Candy

Serving : 24 Cupcakes or a 3 layer 9 inch round cake

INGREDIENTS

Cake Mix

- 3 cups cake flour
- 2 cups sugar
- 2 teaspoons baking soda
- Pinch of salt
- 3 large eggs
- 1-1/2 cups vegetable oil
- 1 teaspoon vinegar
- 1-1/2 cups buttermilk
- 2 tablespoons of cotton candy flavor

Buttercream Frosting

- 4-6 cups confectioners' sugar, sifted
- 1 1/2 ups of unsalted butter, room temperature
- 2 tablespoons vanilla extract
- 1/3 cup heavy cream
- Pinch of salt
- Pink and blue food color
- Garnish with cotton candy

DIRECTIONS

For the Cupcakes:

1. Preheat the oven to 350 degrees —place cupcake papers in a cupcake pan.
2. Sift the cake flour, sugar, salt, and baking soda into a large bowl.
3. In a small mixing bowl, blend eggs and vegetable oil.
4. Mix the buttermilk, vinegar, and cotton candy flavor in a liquid measuring cup.
5. Slowly add the wet ingredients to the dry ingredients while mixing. Mix until combined, scraping the bowl down as needed.
6. Distribute the batter evenly into cupcake papers.
7. Bake at 350 degrees for 20-23 minutes or until springy to the touch.

For the Buttercream Frosting:

1. In a large mixing bowl or the bowl of a stand mixer with the whisk attachment, whip the butter until very light and fluffy, about 5 minutes.
2. Add vanilla, cream, and salt. Mix on low speed until well combined, stopping to scrape down the bowl several times. With the mixer on low, gradually add the confectioners' sugar, about a cup at a time. Scrape down the bowl.
3. Increase the speed to medium-low and beat until fluffy , about 1 minute.
4. Divide the buttercream evenly into two bowls to make the colors blue and pink.
5. Transfer buttercream to a piping bag fitted with a decorative tip and pipe large dollops on top of each cupcake.

Cotton Candy

S'mores

RECIPE CARD

INGREDIENTS:

_____
_____
_____
_____
_____
_____
_____
_____
_____
_____
_____
_____
_____
_____
_____
_____
_____
_____

DIRECTIONS:

_____
_____
_____
_____
_____
_____
_____
_____
_____
_____
_____
_____
_____
_____
_____
_____
_____
_____
_____
_____
_____
_____

Serves   **prep**   **cook**

Notes

RECIPE CARD

INGREDIENTS:

DIRECTIONS:

Serves

prep

cook

Notes

FALL

Pumpkin Spice

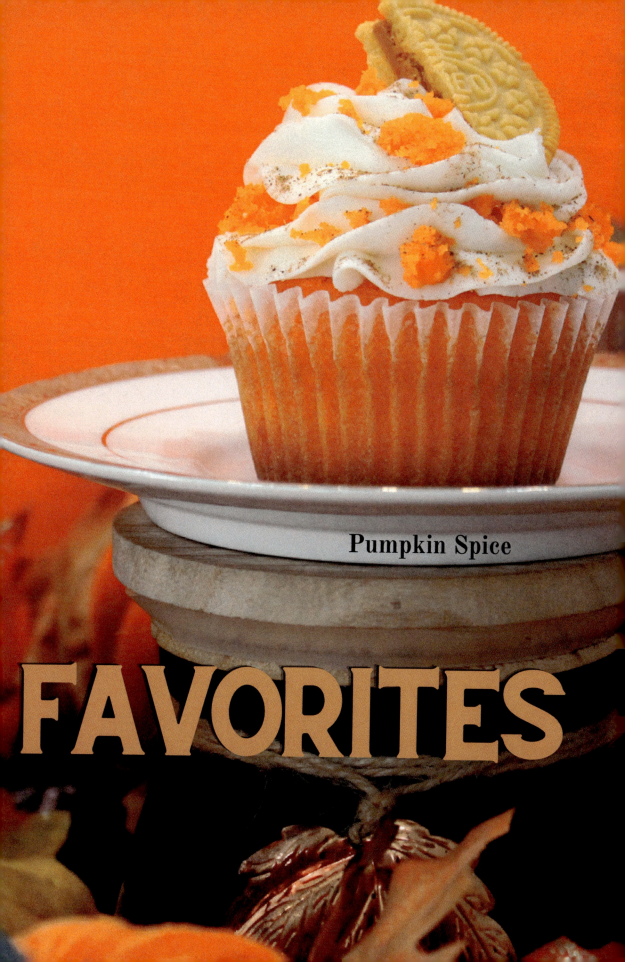

Pumpkin Spice

FAVORITES

PUMPKIN SPICE

Ingredients

Cake Mix
- 3 cups cake flour
- 2 cups sugar
- 2 teaspoons baking soda
- Pinch of salt
- 3 large eggs
- 1-1/2 cups vegetable oil
- 1 teaspoon vinegar
- 1-1/2 cups buttermilk
- 1 teaspoon of pumpkin flavor
- ¼ cup pumpkin pie spice
- 2 teaspoons ground ginger
- 1 teaspoon ground cinnamon
- 1 teaspoon nutmeg

Cream Cheese Frosting
- 1- 8 oz. room-temperature cream cheese
- 3/4 cup of unsalted butter at room temperature
- 1 tsp vanilla extract
- Pinch of salt
- 4 to 6 cups confectioners' sugar, sifted
- Garnish options: ground cinnamon, ground nutmeg, candy corn, or candy pumpkins

Directions

For the Cupcake:
1. Preheat the oven to 350 degrees. Place cupcake papers in a cupcake pan.
2. Sift the cake flour, sugar, salt, pumpkin pie spice, ginger, cinnamon, nutmeg, and baking soda in a large bowl.
3. In a small mixing bowl, blend eggs and vegetable oil.
4. Mix the buttermilk, vinegar, and pumpkin flavor in a liquid measuring cup.
5. Slowly add the wet ingredients to the dry ingredients while mixing. Mix until combined, scraping the sides of the bowl as needed.
6. Distribute the batter evenly into cupcake papers.
7. Bake at 350 degrees for 20-23 minutes or until springy to the touch.

For the Cream Cheese Frosting:
1. In a large mixing bowl or the bowl of a stand mixer fitted with the paddle attachment, beat the butter and cream cheese together on medium speed until smooth and fluffy, about 3 minutes.
2. Add the vanilla and salt and beat until combined.
3. Sift the confectioner's sugar into a large bowl.
4. With the mixer on low speed, gradually add the sugar into the butter mixture until combined. Stop and scrape down the bowl occasionally. Increase speed to medium and beat until fluffy, about 1 minute.
5. Transfer buttercream to a piping bag fitted with a decorative tip and pipe large dollops on top of each cupcake.

APPLE CRUMBLE

Directions

For the Cupcake:

1. Preheat the oven to 350 degrees —place cupcake papers in a cupcake pan.
2. Sift the cake flour, sugar, salt, and baking soda into a large bowl.
3. In a small mixing bowl, blend eggs and vegetable oil.
4. Mix the buttermilk, vinegar, and apple flavor in a liquid measuring cup.
5. Slowly add the wet ingredients to the dry ingredients while mixing. Mix until combined, scraping the bowl down as needed.
6. Distribute the batter evenly into cupcake papers.
7. Bake at 350 degrees for 20-23 minutes or until springy to the touch.

For the Apple Crumble:

1. Preheat the oven to 350 degrees.
2. Combine all ingredients using a fork until thoroughly mixed and crumbly.
3. Toast ingredients on a baking sheet for 7 minutes
4. Sprinkle over your cupcake.

For the Butter Cream Frosting:

1. In a large mixing bowl or the bowl of a stand mixer with the whisk attachment, whip the butter until very light and fluffy, about 5 minutes.
2. Add cream, vanilla and salt. Mix on low speed until well combined, stopping to scrape down the bowl several times. With the mixer on low, gradually add the confectioners' sugar, about a cup at a time. Scrape down the bowl.
3. Increase the speed to medium-low and beat until fluffy, about 1 minute.
4. Transfer buttercream to a piping bag fitted with a decorative tip and pipe large dollops on top of each cupcake.
5. Top the cupcakes with apple pie filling and apple crumble

Ingredients

Cake Mix

- 3 cups cake flour
- 2 cups sugar
- 2 teaspoons baking soda
- Pinch of salt
- 3 large eggs
- 1-1/2 cups vegetable oil
- 1 teaspoon vinegar
- 1-1/2 cups buttermilk
- ¼ cup apple flavor

Butter Cream Frosting

- 4-6 cups confectioners' sugar. sifted
- 1 1/2 cups of unsalted butter, room temperature
- 2 tablespoons vanilla extract
- 1/3 cup heavy cream
- Pinch of salt

Apple Crumble

- 1 cup of flour
- ½ cup brown sugar packed
- ½ cup white sugar
- 1 teaspoon ground cinnamon
- ½ cup butter chilled and cubed

PB&J

Ingredients

Cake Mix
- 3 cups cake flour
- 2 cups sugar
- 2 teaspoons baking soda
- Pinch of salt
- 3 large eggs
- 1-1/2 cups vegetable oil
- 1 teaspoon vinegar
- 1-1/2 cups buttermilk

Buttercream Frosting
- 3 cups confectioners' sugar, sifted
- 1 cup unsalted butter, room temperature
- 1 teaspoon vanilla extract
- 2 tablespoons heavy cream
- 1/2 teaspoon of salt
- 1 cup of creamy peanut butter
- Garnish with strawberry or grape jelly

🍴 24 Cupcakes or a 3 layer 9 inch round cake

Directions

For the Cupcakes:
1. Preheat the oven to 350 degrees —place cupcake papers in a cupcake pan.
2. Sift the cake flour, sugar, salt, and baking soda into a large bowl.
3. In a small mixing bowl, blend eggs and vegetable oil.
4. Mix the buttermilk and vinegar in a liquid measuring cup.
5. Slowly add the wet ingredients to the dry ingredients while mixing. Mix until combined, scraping the bowl down as needed.
6. Distribute the batter evenly into cupcake papers.
7. Bake at 350 degrees for 20-23 minutes or until springy to the touch.
8. Cool cupcakes. Cut a hole in the center of the cupcake and add strawberry or grape jelly filling.

For the Buttercream Frosting:
1. In a large mixing bowl or the bowl of a stand mixer with the scraper attachment, combine butter and peanut butter and mix until well combined.
2. Gradually add confectioners sugar until thoroughly combined with a mixer on low speed. Be sure to scrape the sides of the bowl so all ingredients are well combined.
3. Add vanilla, cream, and salt.
4. Increase the speed to medium-low and beat until fluffy, about 1 minute.
5. Transfer buttercream to a piping bag fitted with a decorative tip and pipe large dollops on top of each cupcake.

CHOCOLATE PEANUT BUTTER

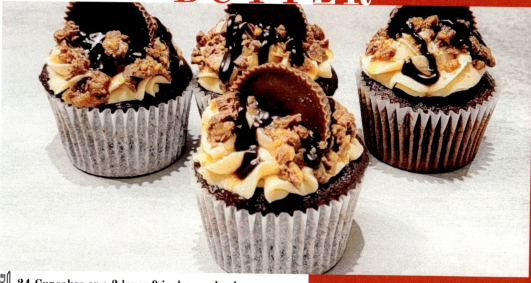

24 Cupcakes or a 3 layer 9 inch round cake

Directions

For the Cupcake:

1. Preheat the oven to 350 degrees —place cupcake papers in a cupcake pan.
2. Sift the cake flour, sugar, salt, cocoa, and baking soda into a large bowl.
3. In a small mixing bowl, blend eggs and vegetable oil. Next, add buttermilk and vinegar.
4. Slowly add the wet ingredients to the dry ingredients while mixing. Mix until combined, scraping the bowl down as needed.
5. Distribute the batter evenly into cupcake papers.
6. Bake at 350 degrees for 20-23 minutes or until springy to the touch.

For the Buttercream Frosting:

1. In a large mixing bowl or the bowl of a stand mixer with the whisk attachment, whip the butter until very light and fluffy, about 5 minutes.
2. Add creamy peanut butter, cream and vanilla. Mix on low speed until well combined, stopping to scrape the sides of the bowl several times. With the mixer on low, gradually add the confectioners' sugar, about a cup at a time. Scrape down the bowl.
3. Increase the speed to medium-low and beat until fluffy, about 1 minute.
4. Transfer buttercream to a piping bag fitted with a decorative tip and pipe large dollops on top of each cupcake.

Ingredients

Cake Mix

- 3 cups cake flour
- 2 cups sugar
- 3 tablespoons of dark cocoa
- 2 teaspoons baking soda
- Pinch of salt
- 3 large eggs
- 1-1/2 cups vegetable oil
- 1 teaspoon vinegar
- 2 cups buttermilk

Peanut Buttercream Frosting

- 1 cup of unsalted butter. room temperature
- 1 cup of creamy peanut butter
- 2 tablespoons of heavy cream
- 3 cups of confectioners' sugar, sifted
- Garnish with peanut butter cups

BANANA PUDDING

Serving : 24 Cupcakes or a 3 layer 9 inch round cake

Ingredients

Cake Mix
- 3 cups cake flour
- 2 cups sugar
- 2 teaspoons baking soda
- Pinch of salt
- 3 large eggs
- 1-1/2 cups vegetable oil
- 1 teaspoon vinegar
- 1-1/2 cups buttermilk
- ¼ cup banana flavor

Buttercream Frosting
- 4-6 cups confectioners' sugar, sifted
- 1 1/2 cups of unsalted butter, room temperature
- 2 tablespoons vanilla extract
- 1/3 cup heavy cream
- Pinch of salt

Banana Pudding Mixture
- 5 oz instant banana-flavored pudding mix
- 2 cups of whole milk
- 14 oz sweetened condensed milk
- 3 cups of whipped cream
- 2 tablespoons of sugar
- 2 teaspoons of vanilla extract

Directions

For the Cupcake:
1. Preheat the oven to 350 degrees —place cupcake papers in a cupcake pan.
2. Sift the cake flour, sugar, salt, and baking soda into a large bowl.
3. In a small mixing bowl, blend eggs and vegetable oil.
4. Mix the buttermilk, vinegar, and banana flavor in a liquid measuring cup.
5. Slowly add the wet ingredients to the dry ingredients while mixing. Mix until combined, scraping the bowl down as needed.
6. Distribute the batter evenly into cupcake papers.
7. Bake at 350 degrees for 20-23 minutes or until springy to the touch.

Banana Pudding:
1. In a large bowl, whisk together the milk and sweetened condensed milk, then sprinkle in the instant pudding and mix until completely incorporated with no lumps remaining. You can do this by hand or with an electric mixer. Refrigerate for 5 minutes or until set.
2. Add 3 cups of whipped cream with two tablespoons of sugar and 2 teaspoons of vanilla to a bowl, then mix on high until stiff peaks form.
3. Remove the pudding from the refrigerator, then fold the whipped cream.
4. Spoon pudding into a piping bag with Wilton tip 1A. Pipe filling into each cooled cupcake.

For the Buttercream Frosting:
1. In a large mixing bowl or the bowl of a stand mixer with the whisk attachment, whip the butter until very light and fluffy, about 5 minutes.
2. Add cream, vanilla, and salt. Mix on low speed until well combined, stopping to scrape down the bowl several times. With the mixer on low, gradually add the confectioners' sugar, about a cup at a time. Scrape down the bowl.
3. Increase the speed to medium-low and beat until fluffy, about 1 minute.
4. Transfer buttercream to a piping bag fitted with a decorative tip and pipe large dollops on top of each cupcake.

GERMAN CHOCOLATE

Ingredients

Cake Mix

- 3 cups cake flour
- 2 cups sugar
- 3 tablespoons of dark cocoa
- 2 teaspoons baking soda
- Pinch of salt
- 3 large eggs
- 1-1/2 cups vegetable oil
- 1 teaspoon vinegar
- 2 cups buttermilk

Coconut-Pecan Filling and Frosting

- 1 12 oz. can of evaporated milk
- 1 1/2 cups sugar
- ¾ cup butter or margarine
- 4 egg yolks
- 1-1/2 teaspoons vanilla extract
- 2-1/3 cups of coconut
- 1-1/2 cups of chopped pecans

Chocolate Butter Cream

- 1 1/2 cups of unsalted butter, room temperature
- ½ cup of unsweetened cocoa
- 3/4 teaspoon salt
- 1-1/2 teaspoons vanilla extract
- 6-8 cups of confectioners' sugar, sifted
- ½ cup of heavy whipping cream

Directions

For the Cake:

1. Preheat the oven to 350 degrees—grease and flour three 9-inch cake pans.
2. Sift the cake flour, sugar, salt, cocoa, and baking soda into a large bowl.
3. In a small mixing bowl, blend eggs, and vegetable oil.
4. Mix the buttermilk and vinegar in a liquid measuring cup.
5. Slowly add the wet ingredients to the dry ingredients while mixing. Mix until combined, scraping the bowl down as needed.
6. Divide the batter among the prepared pans.
7. Bake for about 30 to 35 minutes or until the centers are springy. Let them cool in their pans for about 10 minutes, then turn them onto a wire rack to cool completely.

For the Cupcakes:

1. Preheat oven to 350 degrees. Place cupcake papers in a cupcake pan.
2. Distribute the batter evenly into cupcake papers.
3. Bake at 350 degrees for 20-23 minutes or until springy to the touch.

For the Chocolate Buttercream Frosting:

1. In a large mixing bowl or the bowl of a stand mixer with the whisk attachment, whip the butter until very light and fluffy, about 5 minutes.
2. Add the cocoa powder, vanilla, cream and salt. Mix on low speed until well combined, stopping to scrape the sides of the bowl a couple of times. With the mixer on low, gradually add the confectioners' sugar, about a cup at a time alternating with a tablespoon of cream. (I like 6 cups of sugar for a smooth and swoopy frosting, but I use up to 8 cups of sugar for a stiffer frosting.) Scrape down the bowl.
3. Increase the speed to medium-low and beat until fluffy, about 1 minute. Add additional cream a tablespoon at a time if your frosting feels too thick or stiff.
4. Transfer buttercream to a piping bag fitted with a decorative tip and place large dollops of coconut-pecan filling in the center of each cupcake.

Coconut-Pecan Filling and Frosting

1. Stir milk, sugar, butter, egg yolks, and vanilla in a large saucepan. Stirring constantly; cook on medium heat for 12 minutes or thickened or golden brown. Remove from heat.
2. Stir in coconut and pecans. Cool to room temperature and of spreading consistency.

Butter Pecan

Serving :24 Cupcakes or a 3 layer 9 inch round cake

INGREDIENTS

Cake Mix

- 3 cups cake flour
- 2 cups sugar
- 2 teaspoons baking soda
- Pinch of salt
- 3 large eggs
- 1-1/2 cups vegetable oil
- 1 teaspoon vinegar
- 1-1/2 cups buttermilk
- ¼ cup butter pecan flavor
- 1 cup of finely chopped pecans

Buttercream Frosting

- 4-6 cups confectioners' sugar, sifted
- 1 1/2 cups of unsalted butter, room temperature
- 2 tablespoons vanilla extract
- 1/3 cup heavy cream
- Pinch of salt
- 2 tablespoons of pecan flavor
- Garnish with chopped pecans

DIRECTIONS

For the Cupcake:

1. Preheat the oven to 350 degrees —place cupcake papers in a cupcake pan.
2. Sift the cake flour, sugar, salt, and baking soda into a large bowl.
3. In a small mixing bowl, blend eggs and vegetable oil.
4. Mix the buttermilk, vinegar, and butter pecan flavor in a liquid measuring cup.
5. Slowly add the wet ingredients to the dry ingredients while mixing. Mix until combined, scraping the bowl down as needed. Finally, add finely chopped pecans.
6. Distribute the batter evenly into cupcake papers.
7. Bake at 350 degrees for 20-23 minutes or until springy to the touch.

For the Buttercream Frosting:

1. In a large mixing bowl or the bowl of a stand mixer with the whisk attachment, whip the butter until very light and fluffy, about 5 minutes.
2. Add butter, pecan flavor, cream, vanilla, and salt. Mix on low speed until well combined, stopping to scrape down the bowl several times. With the mixer on low, gradually add the confectioners' sugar, about a cup at a time. Scrape down the bowl.
3. Increase the speed to medium-low and beat until fluffy , about 1 minute.
4. Transfer buttercream to a piping bag fitted with a decorative tip and pipe large dollops on top of each cupcake.

Pistachio

Serving :24 Cupcakes or a 3 layer 9 inch round cake

INGREDIENTS

Cake Mix

- 3 cups cake flour
- 2 cups sugar
- 2 teaspoons baking soda
- Pinch of salt
- 3 large eggs
- 1-1/2 cups vegetable oil
- 1 teaspoon vinegar
- 1-1/2 cups buttermilk
- ¼ cup Pistachio flavor
- 1 cup of finely chopped pistachios
- 2 tablespoons of green food coloring (optional)

Buttercream Frosting

- 4-6 cups of confectioners' sugar, sifted
- 1 1/2 cups of unsalted butter, room temperature
- 2 tablespoons vanilla extract
- 1/3 cup heavy cream
- Pinch of salt
- Optional use 1 drop of leaf green food color
- Garnish with chopped pistachios

DIRECTIONS

For the Cupcake:

1. Preheat the oven to 350 degrees —place cupcake papers in a cupcake pan.
2. Sift the cake flour, sugar, salt, and baking soda into a large bowl.
3. In a small mixing bowl, blend eggs and vegetable oil.
4. Mix the buttermilk, vinegar, and pistachio flavor in a liquid measuring cup.
5. Slowly add the wet ingredients to the dry ingredients while mixing. Mix until combined, scraping the bowl down as needed. Finally, add finely chopped pistachios.
6. Distribute the batter evenly into cupcake papers.
7. Bake at 350 degrees for 20-23 minutes or until springy to the touch.

For the Buttercream Frosting:

1. In a large mixing bowl or the bowl of a stand mixer with the whisk attachment, whip the butter until very light and fluffy, about 5 minutes.
2. Add vanilla, cream and salt. Mix on low speed until well combined, stopping to scrape down the bowl several times. With the mixer on low, gradually add the confectioners' sugar about a cup at a time. Scrape down the bowl. Add green food color.
3. Increase the speed to medium-low and beat until fluffy , about 1 minute.
4. Transfer buttercream to a piping bag fitted with a decorative tip and pipe large dollops on top of each cupcake.

Butter Pecan

RECITE CARD

INGREDIENTS:

_____
_____
_____
_____
_____
_____
_____
_____
_____
_____
_____
_____
_____
_____
_____
_____
_____

DIRECTIONS:

_____
_____
_____
_____
_____
_____
_____
_____
_____
_____
_____
_____
_____
_____
_____
_____
_____
_____
_____
_____
_____
_____
_____

Serves   **prep**   **cook**

Notes

RECIPE CARD

INGREDIENTS:

_____

_____

_____

_____

_____

_____

_____

_____

_____

_____

_____

_____

_____

_____

_____

_____

_____

DIRECTIONS:

_____

_____

_____

_____

_____

_____

_____

_____

_____

_____

_____

_____

_____

_____

_____

_____

_____

_____

_____

_____

Serves

prep

cook

Notes

Orange Creamsicle

Chocolate

Cookie Monster with
edible cookie dough

Yummy

Blue Velevt

year-round

COOKIE MONSTER

Serving: 24 Cupcakes or a 3 layer 9 inch round cake

Ingredients

Cake Mix

- 3 cups cake flour
- 2 cups sugar
- 2 teaspoons baking soda
- Pinch of salt
- 3 large eggs
- 1-1/2 cups vegetable oil
- 1 teaspoon vinegar
- 1-1/2 cups buttermilk
- 1 cup of mini semi-sweet chocolate chips

Buttercream Frosting

- 4-6 cups of confectioners' sugar, sifted
- 1 1/2 cups of unsalted butter, room temperature
- 2 tablespoons vanilla extract
- 1/3 cup heavy cream
- Pinch of salt
- 2 drops of blue food color
- Garnish with chocolate chip cookie

Edible Cookie Dough

- 1 cup all-purpose flour, heat treated to kill bacteria*
- ½ cup unsalted butter softened
- ½ cup packed light brown sugar
- 3 tablespoons granulated sugar
- ¼ teaspoon salt
- 1-1/2 tablespoon milk, then more as needed
- ½ vanilla extract
- ½ cup mini semi-sweet chocolate chips

Directions

For the Cupcakes

1. Preheat the oven to 350 degrees. Place cupcake papers in a cupcake pan. Sift the cake flour, sugar, salt, and baking soda into a large bowl.

2. Mix eggs and vegetable oil in a small mixing bowl.

3. Mix the buttermilk, vinegar, and vanilla in a liquid measuring cup.

4. Slowly add the wet ingredients to the dry ingredients while mixing. Mix until combined, scraping the bowl down as needed. Fold in mini semi-sweet chocolate chips with a spatula.

5. Distribute the batter evenly into cupcake papers.

6. Bake at 350 degrees for 20-23 minutes or until springy to the touch.

For the Buttercream Frosting

1. In a large mixing bowl or the bowl of a stand mixer with the whisk attachment, whip the butter until very light and fluffy, about 5 minutes.

2. Add vanilla, cream, and salt. Mix on low speed until well combined, stopping to scrape down the bowl several times. Add blue food color. With the mixer on low, gradually add the confectioners' sugar, about a cup at a time. Scrape down the bowl.

3. Increase the speed to medium-low and beat until fluffy, about 1 minute.

4. Transfer buttercream to a piping bag fitted with a decorative tip and pipe large dollops on top of each cupcake.

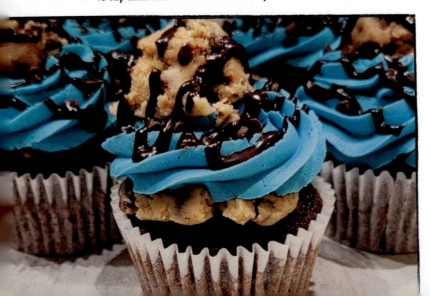

COOKIE BUTTER

Serving: 24 Cupcakes or a 3 layer 9 inch round cake

Ingredients

Cake Mix
- 3 cups cake flour
- 2 cups sugar
- 2 teaspoons baking soda
- Pinch of salt
- 3 large eggs
- 1-1/2 cups vegetable oil
- 1 teaspoon vinegar
- 1-1/2 cups buttermilk
- ¼ cup cookie butter flavor

Buttercram Frosting
- 1 cup of unsalted butter, room temperature
- 1 cup of Bischoff Cookie Butter
- 2 tablespoons vanilla extract
- 1/3 cup of heavy cream
- Pinch of salt
- 5-6 cups of confectioners' sugar, sifted
- Bischoff cookies for topping

Directions

For the Cupcakes

1. Preheat the oven to 350 degrees. Place cupcake papers in a cupcake pan. Sift the cake flour, sugar, salt, and baking soda into a large bowl.

2. Mix eggs and vegetable oil in a small mixing bowl.

3. Mix the buttermilk, vinegar, and cookie butter flavor in a liquid measuring cup.

4. Slowly add the wet ingredients to the dry ingredients while mixing. Mix until combined, scraping the bowl down as needed.

5. Distribute the batter evenly into cupcake papers.

6. Bake at 350 degrees for 20-23 minutes or until springy to the touch.

For the Butter Cream Frosting

1. In a large mixing bowl or the bowl of a stand mixer with the whisk attachment, whip the butter and cookie butter until very light and fluffy, about 5 minutes.

2. Add vanilla, cream, and salt. Mix on low speed until well combined, stopping to scrape down the bowl several times. With the mixer on low, gradually add the sugar about a cup at a time. Scrape down the bowl.

3. Increase the speed to medium-low and beat until fluffy, about 1 minute.

4. Transfer buttercream to a piping bag fitted with a decorative tip and pipe large dollops on top of each cupcake.

Chocolate

CHOCOLATE

Serving :24 Cupcakes or a 3 layer 9 inch round cake

Ingredients

Cake Mix

- 3 cups cake flour
- 2 cups sugar
- 3 tablespoons of dark cocoa
- 2 teaspoons baking soda
- Pinch of salt
- 3 large eggs
- 1-1/2 cups vegetable oil
- 1 teaspoon vinegar
- 2 cups buttermilk

Chocolate Buttercream Frosting

- 1-1/2 cups of unsalted butter, room temperature
- ½ cup of unsweetened cocoa
- ¾ teaspoon of salt
- 1-1/2 teaspoons vanilla extract
- 6-8 cups of confectioners' sugar, sifted
- ½ cup of heavy whipping cream

Directions

For the Cupcake:

1. Preheat the oven to 350 degrees —place cupcake papers in a cupcake pan.
2. Sift the cake flour, sugar, salt, dark cocoa, and baking soda into a large bowl.
3. In a small mixing bowl, blend eggs and vegetable oil.
4. Mix the buttermilk and vinegar in a liquid measuring cup.
5. Slowly add the wet ingredients to the dry ingredients while mixing. Mix until combined, scraping the bowl down as needed.
6. Distribute the batter evenly into cupcake papers.
7. Bake at 350 degrees for 20-23 minutes or until springy to the touch.

For the Chocolate Buttercream Frosting:

1. In a large mixing bowl or the bowl of a stand mixer with the whisk attachment, whip the butter until very light and fluffy, about 3-5 minutes.
2. Add the cocoa, vanilla, cream, and salt. Mix on low speed until well combined, stopping to scrape down the bowl several times. With the mixer on low, gradually add the confectioners' sugar, about a cup, alternating with a tablespoon of cream. (I like 6 cups of sugar for a smooth and swoopy frosting but for a stiffer frosting, use up to 8 cups of sugar.) Scrape down the bowl.
3. Increase the speed to medium-low and beat until fluffy, about 1 minute.
4. Transfer buttercream to a piping bag fitted with a decorative tip and pipe large dollops on top of each cupcake.

BUBBLE GUM

Serving :24 Cupcakes or a 3 layer 9 inch round cake

Ingredients

Cake Mix
- 3 cups cake flour
- 2 cups sugar
- 2 teaspoons baking soda
- Pinch of salt
- 3 large eggs
- 1-1/2 cups vegetable oil
- 1 teaspoon vinegar
- 1-1/2 cups buttermilk
- 2 tablespoons bubble gum flavor

Buttercream Frosting
- 4-6 cups confectioners' sugar, sifted
- 1 1/2 cups of unsalted butter. room temperature
- 2 tablespoons vanilla extract
- 1/3 cup heavy cream
- Pinch of salt
- Blue food color
- Pink food color
- Garnish with colorful bubble gum balls

Directions

For the Cupcakes:
1. Preheat the oven to 350 degrees.
2. Place cupcake papers in a cupcake pan.
3. Sift the cake flour, sugar, salt, and baking soda into a large bowl.
4. Mix eggs and vegetable oil in a small mixing bowl.
5. Mix the buttermilk, vinegar, and bubble gum flavor in a liquid measuring cup.
4. Slowly add the wet ingredients to the dry ingredients while mixing. Mix until combined, scraping the bowl down as needed.
5. Distribute the batter evenly into cupcake papers.
6. Bake at 350 degrees for 20-23 minutes or until springy to the touch.

For the Buttercream Frosting:
1. In a large mixing bowl or the bowl of a stand mixer with the whisk attachment, whip the butter until very light and fluffy, about 5 minutes.
2. Add cream and salt. Mix on low speed until well combined, stopping to scrape down the bowl several times. With the mixer on low, gradually add the sugar, about a cup at a time. Scrape down the bowl.
3. Increase the speed to medium-low and beat until fluffy, about 1 minute.
4. Divide the buttercream evenly into two bowls to make the colors blue and pink.
5. Transfer buttercream to a piping bag fitted with a decorative tip and pipe large dollops on top of each cupcake.

Bubblegum

ROLO ®

Directions

For the Cupcakes:

1. Preheat the oven to 350 degrees and place cupcake papers in a cupcake pan.
2. Sift the cake flour, sugar, salt, and baking soda into a large bowl.
3. In a small mixing bowl, blend eggs and vegetable oil.
4. Mix the buttermilk and vinegar in a liquid measuring cup.
5. Slowly add the wet ingredients to the dry ingredients while mixing. Mix until combined, scraping the bowl down as needed. Stir in finely chopped Rolo candies
6. Distribute the batter evenly into cupcake papers.
7. Bake at 350 degrees for 20-23 minutes or until springy to the touch.

For the Buttercream Frosting:

1. In a large mixing bowl or the bowl of a stand mixer with the whisk attachment, whip the butter until very light and fluffy, about 5 minutes.
2. Add vanilla, cream, and salt. Mix on low speed until well combined, stopping to scrape down the bowl several times. With the mixer on low, gradually add the confectioners' sugar about a cup at a time. Scrape down the bowl.
3. Increase the speed to medium-low and beat until fluffy, about 1 minute. Fold in Rolo candies by hand using a spatula.
4. Transfer buttercream to a piping bag fitted with a decorative tip and pipe large dollops on top of each cupcake.

For the Caramel Sauce:

1. Add the sugar and water into a medium saucepan and stir until the sugar is dissolved. Place over medium-high heat and brush the pot inside with a wet pastry brush, so crystals do not form.
2. Cook until the sugar mixture becomes golden amber, remove from heat, and whisk in the cream vigorously. Add butter and bring back to medium-low heat. Continue whisking and cook for an additional 2-3 minutes.
3. Mix in salt, transfer to a bowl and set aside to cool to room temperature.

🍴 24 Cupcakes or a 3 layer 9 inch round cake

Ingredients

Cake Mix

- 3 cups cake flour
- 2 cups sugar
- 2 teaspoons baking soda
- Pinch of salt
- 3 large eggs
- 1-1/2 cups vegetable oil
- 1 teaspoon vinegar
- 1-1/2 cups buttermilk
- 2 cups of finely chopped Rolo candies

Buttercream Frosting

- 4-6 cups confectioners' sugar, sifted
- 1 1/2 cups of unsalted butter, room temperature
- 2 tablespoons vanilla extract
- 1/3 cup heavy cream
- Pinch of salt
- Garnish with Rolo and homemade caramel sauce

Easy Caramel Sauce

- 1-1/2 cups sugar
- ¼ cup water
- 1 cup heavy cream
- 5 tablespoons unsalted butter
- ½ teaspoons salt

SNICKERS ®

Serving: 24 Cupcakes or a 3 layer 9 inch round cake

Ingredients

Cake Mix

- 3 cups cake flour
- 2 cups sugar
- 3 tablespoons of dark cocoa
- 2 teaspoons baking soda
- Pinch of salt
- 3 large eggs
- 1-1/2 cups vegetable oil
- 1 teaspoon vinegar
- 2 cups buttermilk
- 2 cups of finely chopped snickers

Buttercream Frosting

- 4-6 cups confectioners' sugar, sifted
- 1 1/2 cups of unsalted butter, room temperature
- 2 tablespoons vanilla extract
- 1/3 cup heavy cream
- Pinch of salt
- Garnish with Snickers and caramel sauce

Directions

For the Cupcakes:

1. Preheat the oven to 350 degrees — place cupcake papers in a cupcake pan.
2. Sift the cake flour, sugar, salt, cocoa, and baking soda into a large bowl.
3. In a small mixing bowl, blend eggs and vegetable oil.
4. Mix the buttermilk and vinegar. Slowly add the wet ingredients to the dry ingredients while mixing. Mix until combined, scraping the bowl down as needed.
6. Distribute the batter evenly into cupcake papers.
7. Bake at 350 degrees for 20-23 minutes or until springy to the touch.

For the Butter Cream Frosting:

1. In a large mixing bowl or the bowl of a stand mixer with the whisk attachment, whip the butter until very light and fluffy, about 5 minutes.
2. Add vanilla, cream, and salt. Mix on low speed until well combined, stopping to scrape down the bowl several times. With the mixer on low, gradually add the confectioners' sugar about a cup at a time. Scrape down the bowl.
3. Increase the speed to medium-low and beat until fluffy, about 1 minute. Fold in snickers by hand using a spatula.
4. Transfer buttercream to a piping bag fitted with a decorative tip and pipe large dollops on top of each cupcake.

Chocolate Honeycomb

Better Than Anything

Serving: 24 Cupcakes or a 3 layer 9 inch round cake

INGREDIENTS

Cake Mix

- 3 cups cake flour
- 2 cups sugar
- 3 tablespoons of dark cocoa
- 2 teaspoons baking soda
- Pinch of salt
- 3 large eggs
- 1-1/2 cups vegetable oil
- 1 teaspoon vinegar
- 2 cups buttermilk

Caramel sauce

- 1 can sweetened condensed milk
- ¾ cup caramel sauce

Buttercream Frosting

- 4-6 cups of confectioners' sugar, sifted
- 1 1/2 cup of unsalted butter. room temperature
- 2 tablespoons vanilla extract
- 1/3 cup heavy cream
- Pinch of salt

DIRECTIONS

For the Cupcakes:

1. Preheat the oven to 350 degrees—place cupcake papers in a cupcake pan.
2. Sift together the cake flour, sugar, salt, cocoa, and baking soda in a large bowl.
3. In a small mixing bowl, blend eggs and vegetable oil.
4. Mix the buttermilk and vinegar in a liquid measuring cup.
5. Slowly add the wet ingredients to the dry ingredients while mixing. Mix until combined, scraping the bowl down as needed.
6. Distribute the batter evenly into cupcake papers.
7. Bake at 350 degrees for 20-23 minutes or until springy to the touch.
8. Take the end of a wooden chopstick, poke the middle and move it around a bit to make a hole.
9. Once the hole is formed, take your squirt bottle filled with caramel sauce and squeeze a generous amount into the cupcake. Let it cool completely.

For the Buttercream Frosting:

1. In a large mixing bowl or the bowl of a stand mixer with the whisk attachment, whip the butter until very light and fluffy, about 5 minutes.
2. Add vanilla, cream and salt. Mix on low speed until well combined, stopping to scrape down the bowl several times. With the mixer on low, gradually add the confectioners' sugar, about a cup at a time. (I like 6 cups of sugar for a smooth and swoopy frosting, (I use up to 8 cups of sugar for a stiffer frosting.) Scrape down the bowl.
3. Increase the speed to medium-low and beat until fluffy, about 1 minute.
4. Transfer buttercream to a piping bag fitted with a decorative tip and pipe large dollops on top of each cupcake.
5. Garnish with caramel and chocolate sauce and top with milk chocolate Heath bits.

Chocolate Honeycomb

Serving: 24 Cupcakes or a 3 layer 9 inch round cake

INGREDIENTS

Cake Mix

- 3 cups cake flour
- 2 cups sugar
- 3 tablespoons dark cocoa
- 2 teaspoons baking soda
- Pinch of salt
- 3 large eggs
- 1-1/2 cups vegetable oil
- 1 teaspoon vinegar

Easy Honey Buttercream

- 4-6 cups of confectioners' sugar, sifted
- 1 1/2 cup of unsalted butter, room temperature
- 1/3 cup honey
- 1/2 teaspoon vanilla extract
- Pinch of salt
- Yellow food color
- Garnish with honeycomb cereal, drizzle with honey

DIRECTIONS

For the Cupcakes:

1. Preheat the oven to 350 degrees —place cupcake papers in a cupcake pan.
2. Sift the cake flour, sugar, salt, cocoa, and baking soda into a large bowl.
3. In a small mixing bowl, blend eggs and vegetable oil.
4. Mix the buttermilk and vinegar in a liquid measuring cup.
5. Slowly add the wet ingredients to the dry ingredients while mixing. Mix until combined, scraping the bowl down as needed.
6. Distribute the batter evenly into cupcake papers.
7. Bake at 350 degrees for 20-23 minutes or until springy to the touch.

For Buttercream:

1. In a large mixing bowl or the bowl of a stand mixer with the whisk attachment, whip the butter until very light and fluffy, about 5 minutes.
2. Add honey, cream, vanilla, yellow food color, and salt. Mix on low speed until well combined, stopping to scrape down the bowl several times. With the mixer on low, gradually add the confectioner's sugar, about a cup at a time. Scrape down the bowl.
3. Increase the speed to medium-low and beat until fluffy, about 1 minute.
4. Transfer buttercream to a piping bag fitted with a decorative tip and pipe large dollops on top of each cupcake. Garnish with cereal and drizzle with honey.

VANILLA SPRINKLES

Serving :24 Cupcakes or a 3 layer 9 inch round cake

Ingredients

Cake Mix

- 3 cups cake flour
- 2 cups sugar
- 2 teaspoons baking soda
- Pinch of salt
- 3 large eggs
- 1-1/2 cups vegetable oil
- 1 teaspoon vinegar
- 1-1/2 cups buttermilk
- 2 tablespoon vanilla extract
- Optional 1 cup of rainbow sprinkles

Buttercream Frosting

- 4-6 cups confectioners' sugar, sifted
- 1 1/2 cups unsalted butter, room temperature
- 2 tablespoons vanilla extract
- 1/3 cup heavy cream
- Pinch of salt
- Garnish with rainbow sprinkles, teddy grahams and splash of sweet milk

Directions

For the Cupcakes:

1. Preheat the oven to 350 degrees.
2. Place cupcake papers in a cupcake pan.
3. Sift the cake flour, sugar, salt, and baking soda into a large bowl.
4. Mix eggs and vegetable oil in a small mixing bowl.
5. Mix the buttermilk, vanilla, and vinegar in a liquid measuring cup.
6. Slowly add the wet ingredients to the dry ingredients while mixing. Mix until combined, scraping the bowl down as needed.
7. Distribute the batter evenly into cupcake papers.
8. Bake at 350 degrees for 20-23 minutes or until springy to the touch.

For the Buttercream Frosting:

1. In a large mixing bowl or the bowl of a stand mixer with the whisk attachment, whip the butter until very light and fluffy, about 5 minutes.
2. Add vanilla, cream, and salt. Mix on low speed until well combined, stopping to scrape down the bowl several times. With the mixer on low, gradually add the confectioner's sugar, about a cup at a time. Scrape down the bowl.
3. Increase the speed to medium-low and beat until fluffy, about 1 minute.
4. Transfer buttercream to a piping bag fitted with a decorative tip and pipe large dollops on top of each cupcake.

Vanilla with Sprinkles

RECIPE CARD

INGREDIENTS:

_____
_____
_____
_____
_____
_____
_____
_____
_____
_____
_____
_____
_____
_____
_____
_____
_____
_____
_____

Serves   **prep**   **cook**

DIRECTIONS:

_____
_____
_____
_____
_____
_____
_____
_____
_____
_____
_____
_____
_____
_____
_____
_____
_____
_____
_____
_____
_____

Notes

RECIPE CARD

INGREDIENTS:

_____
_____
_____
_____
_____
_____
_____
_____
_____
_____
_____
_____
_____
_____
_____
_____
_____

DIRECTIONS:

_____
_____
_____
_____
_____
_____
_____
_____
_____
_____
_____
_____
_____
_____
_____

Serves

prep

cook

Notes

Rum Raisin

White Chocolate Surprise

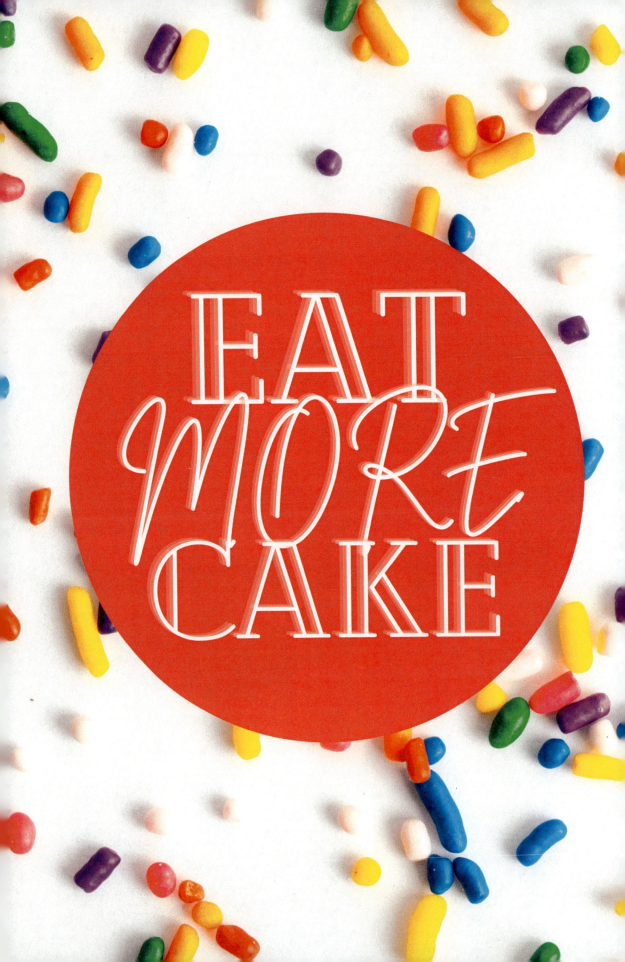

Made in the USA
Middletown, DE
23 September 2023

39174802R00044